BENITO JUAREZ

PRESIDENT OF MEXICO

FRANK DE VARONA

Consultants:

Dr. Julian Nava
Historian
Former U.S. Ambassador to Mexico

Yolanda Quintanilla-Finley
Teacher and Project Specialist
Corona Unified School District
Corona, California

Hispanic Heritage
The Millbrook Press
Brookfield, Connecticut

Published by The Millbrook Press
2 Old New Milford Road
Brookfield, Connecticut 06804

Cover photo courtesy of UPI/Bettmann

Map by Joe LeMonnier

Photos courtesy of Culver Pictures: pp. 3, 6, 7, 13;
Bettmann Archives: pp. 9, 17, 23, 24, 29; AP/Wide
World Photos: pp. 10, 11; Mexican Consulate: pp. 15,
20, 25, 28; Bridgeman/Art Resource: p. 27.

Library of Congress Cataloging-in-Publication Data

De Varona, Frank.
Benito Juárez, President of Mexico / by Frank de Varona.
p. cm.—(Hispanic heritage)
Summary: Presents the life of the Zapotec Indian who officially
became president of Mexico in 1861, instituted many reforms, and led
his country in a war of independence.
ISBN 1-56294-279-4 (lib. bdg.)
1. Juárez, Benito, 1806–1872—Juvenile literature.   2. Mexico—
History—1821–1861—Juvenile literature.   3. Mexico—History—
European intervention, 1861–1867—Juvenile literature.
4. Presidents—Mexico—Biography—Juvenile literature.   [1. Juárez,
Benito, 1806–1872.   2. Presidents—Mexico.   3. Zapotec Indians—
Biography.   4. Indians of Mexico—Biography.]   I. Title.
II. Series.
F1233.J9D4   1993
972'.07'092—dc20
[B]   92-19349   CIP   AC

BENITO JUAREZ

High in the mountains in Mexico's southern state of Oaxaca (pronounced Wah-HAH-kah) lay a tiny village called San Pablo Guelatao. The people of Guelatao were Zapotec Indians. They had come to the region more than two thousand years before. It was a quiet and peaceful place set off from the rest of the country by the great mountain range called the Sierra del Sur. Life for the Indians of Guelatao was simple, but it was also hard.

Here in Guelatao, on March 21, 1806, Benito Pablo Juárez, the future president of Mexico, was born. His mother was a Zapotec Indian named Brígida García. His father was named Marcelino Juárez. The family lived in a two-room house with a dirt floor.

When Benito was born, Spain had been ruling Mexico for almost three hundred years. Mexico was part of a much larger region called the Viceroyalty of New Spain. This Spanish empire in the Americas included much of the western and southern parts of the United States. It stretched through Mexico, Central America, the Caribbean islands, and all the way down to the southern tip of South America.

The king of Spain ruled over this huge area. But he lived 4,000 miles (6,400 kilometers) away in Spain's capital city of Madrid. So, he chose a Spanish official called a viceroy to rule over New Spain in his place.

Many different races of people lived together there. They were divided into classes according to their origin.

Sitting in front of their homes, Indian women shell dried corn—an ancient Mayan practice.

Facing page: An Indian boy in Mexico.

At the top were the people born in Spain. They were called *peninsulares*. Only Spanish men could be high officials in the government, the church, and the military. Next in wealth and power were people born of Spanish parents in Mexico or in some other part of the Spanish empire. They were called *Creoles*. Many Spaniards and Creoles had children with American Indians. These children were known as *mestizos*. Both Creoles and mestizos thought that they were better than full-blooded Indians.

Indians were the lowest on the social scale, except for the Africans, who lived in slavery. They tended to live apart from the rest of the people. Since they were almost never offered good jobs, they lived in terrible poverty. Most of their children did not even have the chance to go to school. This was the world into which Benito Juárez was born.

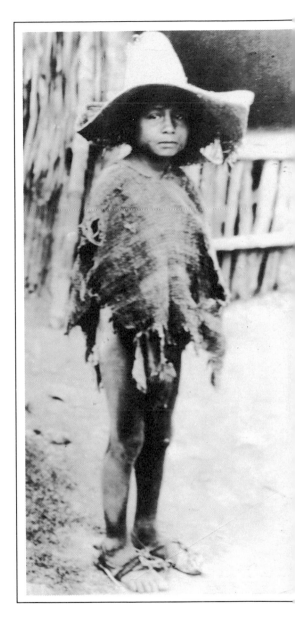

A BRIEF CHILDHOOD · Like most Indians, Benito's parents were poor and uneducated. Then Benito's mother died in childbirth. When Benito was three years old, his father died, too.

Benito and his three sisters went to live with their grandfather. But within a few years, he also died. Benito was taken in by his uncle Bernardino Juárez. His sisters went to live with other relatives.

Benito spent most of his time working in Bernardino's fields and tending his sheep. He learned to be patient. And he learned to be responsible and brave because shepherds had to protect their animals from mountain lions and other dangers.

Benito loved his uncle. Bernardino told him the history of the Zapotecs. Benito learned that they had been great kings, astronomers, and poets before they were conquered by the Spaniards. Throughout his life, Benito would be proud of his Indian heritage.

Like other Indians in his village, Benito's uncle was not an educated man. But he taught his nephew all he knew. As Benito grew older, though, he wanted to learn more than his uncle could teach him. Everyone in the village spoke Zapotec, an Indian language, and Benito wanted to learn to speak and write Spanish. He knew that if he wanted to succeed, he would have to go to the city to continue his education. But the decision to leave his uncle and his friends was very hard for him.

When the Spanish conquered Mexico they destroyed its ancient civilizations. Here, conquistadores pull down a Mexican religious sculpture.

Then one day in December 1818, Benito was tending his uncle's sheep when a group of strangers walked over and started talking to him. After they had gone, Benito realized that the men had stolen one of his sheep. He was afraid that his uncle would punish him, and he was probably also looking for an excuse to leave his village.

Whatever the reason, at dawn the next day, the twelve-year-old boy set out alone on the 40-mile (64-kilometer) walk down the mountains to Oaxaca city. As he walked down the steep path from his village that day, Benito left behind his childhood forever.

ZAPOTEC INDIANS: PEOPLE OF THE CLOUDS

Zapotec Indians came to the southern Mexican state of Oaxaca about 2,500 years ago. They built royal palaces, public buildings, and plazas in the mountaintop city of Monte Albán.

Over the centuries, the Zapotecs built other capital cities such as Mitla. They dug canals for crop irrigation in the valleys, and they carved statues and recorded their military victories on stones called conquest slabs. Zapotec Indians call themselves an ancient name, *benezaa* or *vinizaa*, meaning "people of the clouds."

Zapotecs still live in towns and farming villages in southern Mexico. They are known for their fine pottery and woven goods. Many still speak the Zapotec Indian language. They are proud of their Native American traditions and of Benito Juárez, the hero of Mexico who came from their midst.

These are the ruins of the huge Zapotec city at Monte Albán, which flourished from about A.D. 500 through the early 1200s.

The cathedral in Oaxaca, the city that for Benito signified entry into a larger world.

INDEPENDENCE · Luckily Benito had somewhere to go in the city. His older sister, María Josefa, lived in the home of an Italian family, where she worked as a cook. Somehow Benito, with his limited Spanish, made his way through the dark city streets to the house of Antonio Maza. He was welcomed in and given a straw mat in the servant's room on which to sleep.

Benito soon found a job as a houseboy for Don Antonio Salanueva, a very wealthy and religious man who worked as a bookbinder. Benito's new home was full of books, but he still could not read them.

Don Antonio, who was very fond of Benito, adopted him and enrolled him in an elementary school. There, Benito experienced prejudice for the first time. The Indian students were treated differently from the wealthy Spanish children. They were even taught in separate classes—by the worst teachers in the school.

Benito's teacher had no patience with him and punished him when he made mistakes. Benito was angry and hurt that he was not given a fair chance to learn. Years later he wrote, "I decided to leave school and practice by myself the little I had learned, until I could express my ideas in writing—however poor the form might be, as it is to this day."

Each day he cleaned Don Antonio's house. Then he read, wrote, and studied late into the night. He also loved to play. He swam in a nearby lake with other boys and visited the ruins of Monte Albán, the remains of the great achievements of the Zapotec Indian culture.

He learned about how his people had been pushed to the bottom of society when the Spanish took control of Mexico. He became aware of the great anger felt by all Mexicans—Creoles, mestizos, and his fellow Indians—toward their Spanish rulers. He learned that several people had tried to break free from Spain's grip in recent years, but so far they had not been successful. Part of the problem was that the different races had been unable to join together behind one leader.

FATHER HIDALGO AND THE GRITO DE DOLORES

A creole priest named Miguel Hidalgo y Costilla led the first Mexican revolt against Spanish rule. Father Hidalgo was an educated man who was familiar with the European thinkers who questioned the right of kings and queens to control the lives of other people.

At about two o'clock in the morning on September 16, 1810, Hidalgo called the mestizos and Indians of the village of Dolores to his church. He made a speech that became known as the *Grito de Dolores* (the Cry of Dolores), the battle cry of the Mexican Revolution.

With an army of about 50,000 men, Hidalgo captured several cities, including Guadalajara, where the revolutionaries set up a new government.

Almost a year later, Hidalgo was captured and shot. Ten years would go by before Mexico would be free. But to this day, early in the morning on September 16, the bells in Mexico's churches ring, and officials repeat the *Grito de Dolores* in memory of Father Hidalgo and his fight for freedom.

As the world of ideas opened up for Benito, he became even more eager to break out of his own position in society. He noticed that the young men who went to the local religious seminary to prepare for the priesthood were treated with great respect by the people of Oaxaca. Don Antonio encouraged him to enroll.

In 1821, Benito Juárez began his religious studies. In that same year Mexico finally won its independence from Spain under a creole general named Agustín de Iturbide. For Mexico, though, freedom from Spain would not bring peace for the nation.

RISING HIGHER · By 1828, Juárez had graduated from the seminary, but he decided to become a lawyer instead of a priest. At the age of twenty-two he began to study at the Institute of Arts and Sciences, a government college. He continued to work very hard. One day a teacher pointed out Juárez to the other students, saying, "This one here, who's so serious and reserved, will be a great politician. He will rise higher than any of us, and he will be one of our great men and the glory of our country!"

Juárez was still a student at the college in 1829 when a creole general named Antonio López de Santa Anna arrived in Oaxaca. The college gave a banquet in his honor, and Juárez, who worked as a waiter, served the general. In later years the two men would become bitter enemies.

Antonio López de Santa Anna, legendary general and dictator of Mexico, was the lifelong enemy of Benito Juárez.

In 1831, Juárez began working as a lawyer. He was elected to the Oaxaca city council, and two years later, he was elected to the Oaxaca state legislature, its lawmaking body, as a Liberal party member.

The government in Mexico had been in constant change since the country became independent. The two main political parties in power in the early days of the republic were the Conservatives and the Liberals. The Conservatives were backed by the Catholic Church and wealthy creole landowners and merchants.

The Catholic Church was extremely wealthy. It had more money than the government, but it paid no taxes. It charged money for religious services such as baptisms, confessions, marriages, and burials. And by law, all members had to make regular payments, whose amounts were decided by the church. Priests and high church officials were very powerful. If accused of a crime, they, like the military, were tried in their own special court.

Juárez and other Liberals believed that the Catholic Church was too powerful. When the Liberal party took over in the 1830s, it declared that soldiers and church officials were to be tried in civil courts along with the rest of the people. Mexican citizens did not have to pay money to the church anymore either. The army, the church, the Conservative party, and wealthy landowners rose up against the Liberal government. As a member of the Liberal party, Juárez was arrested. But he was soon released. General Santa Anna had led the revolt.

Juárez returned to his law practice and his defense of poor people and Indians. In 1834 villagers from Loricha asked him to defend them from their priest, who made them pay huge sums of money to their church.

Juárez took their case to court. The judge sided with the priest. He arrested the young lawyer as well as many of the villagers. Juárez spent nine days in jail. This injustice and other abuses that Juárez saw around him only strengthened his desire to fight.

Benito Juárez with an open book, symbolizing his strong belief in the law as the way to bring justice to his country.

Juárez, now a lawyer and a politician, continued his friendship with the Maza family. He did not forget how they had taken him in when he was a boy. In 1843 he married Doña Margarita Maza, whom he had known as a little girl and watched grow up into a beautiful woman. He was thirty-seven and Margarita was seventeen. They had twelve children, nine girls and three boys. Three of the girls died as babies, and two of the boys died when they were very young. Despite these sorrows, they had a very happy marriage. Margarita loved her husband deeply and stood by him throughout his difficult life.

GOVERNOR OF OAXACA · In 1846 the United States and Mexico declared war. Earlier, Mexico had lost Texas. The Texans had declared their independence and defeated General Santa Anna's army from Mexico. In 1845 the United States Congress voted to annex Texas—to make Texas part of the United States. Mexico refused to recognize this action. Soon there was a dispute about the boundary between Texas and Mexico. This led to war. When the war ended in 1848, Mexico had lost half of its territory to the United States.

During this time, Juárez was elected to represent the state of Oaxaca in the national legislature. He served one year. Then, in 1847, he was appointed governor of the state of Oaxaca. The following year he was elected to the same position.

Juárez was an outstanding governor. He built schools and roads. He stopped government officials from stealing from the people; he made them work for their money instead.

MINISTER OF JUSTICE · When his term ended in 1852, Juárez returned to his law practice. The following year Conservative general Santa Anna became president of Mexico. He hated Liberals, especially Juárez. One day Juárez was arrested and sent to jail. He spent several months in prison even though he had committed no crime. Then in 1853 he was sent into exile—that is, forced to leave his country against his will.

Juárez lived in New Orleans with other Mexican exiles until 1855 when he returned to Mexico and pushed the Conservative government of Santa Anna out. Juárez became minister of justice, the most powerful lawmaker in the country.

He worked hard to bring reforms to Mexico. One of his laws was called *Ley Juárez*, the Juárez Law. It ended the system of separate courts for the army and the church for good. Now all Mexicans were equal before the law. Another law forced the church to sell most of its properties. Juárez's most important achievement was the writing of the Constitution of 1857, which included many needed reforms. That same year Juárez was elected president of the Supreme Court, the highest court in the land.

Juárez holds his triumph, the Constitution of 1857, which brought many important reforms to Mexico.

Then, on January 11, 1858, Mexico again erupted in civil war. The church and the army rose up against the Liberals. While many Liberals, including the president, left the country, Juárez refused to quit. He fled from Mexico City, walking from farm to farm and even sleeping in fields at night. As head of the Supreme Court, Juárez was also vice president of Mexico. When he reached the safety of a mining town in the mountains, he declared himself president.

That was how a fifty-two-year-old Zapotec Indian, born in poverty and orphaned at the age of three, became the president of his country. But declaring himself president and keeping in power were two very different things.

PRESIDENT OF MEXICO · Within a few days, President Juárez and his supporters moved the government to the city of Guadalajara. But a group of soldiers captured Juárez and members of his government. The soldiers raised their rifles and the officer yelled, "Ready! Aim!" A young man threw himself in front of Juárez and cried, "Put up your arms! Brave men are not assassins! You want blood? Take mine!" As the story goes, the soldiers lowered their rifles and wept. Juárez was saved.

The new president moved to Veracruz, where he continued to fight. Through his iron will, patience, and courage, Juárez led his army to victory. In 1860 he returned to Mexico City in triumph. The following year his presidency was officially confirmed. However, his troubles were far from over.

During the years of civil war, Mexico had borrowed heavily from France, England, and Spain. Now Mexico was deeply in debt. Juárez demanded that Mexico be given two years in which to repay this money. But France, England, and Spain decided to send their armies to collect their debts instead.

The United States was against this action, but its own bloody civil war kept it from coming to Mexico's aid. Eventually England and Spain withdrew their armies, but France did not. The French emperor Napoleon III dreamed of ruling over Mexico. Conservative Mexican leaders supported him. They saw in French rule the chance to overthrow the Liberal government.

Maximilian, the twenty-nine-year-old brother of Emperor Francis Joseph of Austria, was eager to come to Mexico to rule in Napoleon's name. Conservatives told Maximilian and his wife, Carlota, daughter of the king of Belgium, that the Mexican people wanted an emperor. Maximilian foolishly believed them.

President Juárez was forced, once again, to flee from Mexico City. Just before the French army arrived, he ordered that all important government papers be packed. He then brought his ministers to the presidential palace. While the army band played the national anthem, the flag was lowered and given to the president. He accepted it, kissed it, and cried out "Viva Mexico!" Then Juárez, his army, and his officials took flight.

WAR TO DEATH! · The new emperor of Mexico, Maximilian, and his wife, Carlota, landed in Veracruz on May 28, 1864. Carlota was very disappointed that there were no cheering masses waiting to greet them. Maximilian was a well-meaning, though ill-informed, nobleman who wanted to improve the lives of the Mexican people. Carlota longed for glory and power. Neither realized that most Mexicans saw them as invaders supported by the hated French army.

Maximilian then started to anger his supporters, the Conservatives. He had liberal ideas, and he even wrote several letters to Juárez asking him to join his government. Juárez replied, "When a foreigner intervenes in our affairs with bayonets, we shall make war on him to death."

Maximilian was emperor of Mexico for three years. Napoleon III used him, without success, to gain influence in North America.

Maximilian's wife, Carlota, was a headstrong woman of great ambition.

The new emperor ordered seven portraits of himself. The emperor and empress gave seventy luncheons, twenty banquets, sixteen balls, and twelve receptions during the first six months of their reign. They spent huge amounts of money on wine and champagne at a time when the country was torn apart by civil war and hopelessly in debt to European powers.

The French armies continued to attack and defeat the Liberals. The president was forced to retreat farther and farther north to escape. Again Juárez relied on his patience and loyalty. No matter how bad the odds against him, he did not give up.

Juárez and his outnumbered troops battled the French and, in the end, were victorious.

Finally he arrived at El Paso del Norte (today, called Ciudad Juárez in his honor). This city was more than 1,000 miles (1,600 kilometers) from Mexico City and right next to the border with the United States. Juárez had hardly any money to buy weapons. His army had met defeat after defeat. Some of his generals had left the country or joined the French. He and his small army faced 35,000 French soldiers. Yet Juárez did not retreat.

Slowly his army began pushing back the French. In 1866, a year after the American Civil War ended in the United States, Secretary of State William Seward again demanded that the French get out of Mexico. U.S. president Andrew Johnson ordered 50,000 American soldiers to the Texas border to pressure Napoleon III.

France was also worried that it would soon have to fight a European war against Prussia (now Germany). French troops were needed back in France. In 1867, Napoleon III told Maximilian that he had decided to withdraw the French army from Mexico. He advised Maximilian to give up the throne of Mexico and return to Europe.

Maximilian agreed. But Carlota would not give up. She went to Paris to beg Napoleon to help them. When he refused to budge, she went straight to the pope, the head of the Catholic Church in Rome. He would do nothing for them.

Many historians say that Carlota's disappointment was so great that she went mad. Carlota believed that she was poisoned. What is certain is that from that point on she suffered from a nervous disorder. Unable to manage by herself, she was taken back to Belgium.

Maximilian was shot in Mexico on June 19, 1867. Carlota lived on, never fully recovered, until her death in 1927.

Edouard Manet's painting of Emperor Maximilian's execution.

After a four-year absence, Benito Juárez returns to Mexico City, the beloved hero of his people.

A TRIUMPHANT RETURN · On July 15, 1867, Benito Juárez entered Mexico City to the wild cheering of his people. His leadership was respected and admired. He was elected to a third term as president in 1867 and later elected to a fourth term in 1871.

President Juárez began the great task of rebuilding a country destroyed by years of civil war and foreign military invasions. He did his best to unite the Mexican people. The government built schools and roads and improved the lives of the poor. A railroad was built between Mexico City and Veracruz.

Then, in 1871, the president's beloved wife, Margarita, died at the age of forty-four. Her death was a terrible blow to Juárez. For a month, he was unable to work at all. On July 18 of the following year, he suffered a heart attack. The doctor ordered him to rest. But Juárez kept working in his bed until late that night. He died in his sleep just before midnight.

Benito Juárez had refused to let up, even for a moment, on his undying love for his country. His country loved him in return. He was their hero, a great lawmaker and statesman who saved Mexico from foreign control and did his best to bring justice to its people.

To this day, Mexicans honor him, as do people throughout Latin America, by calling him *Benemérito de las Américas*— "worthy hero of the Americas."

Memorial to President Benito Juárez, who was born a poor outcast and grew up to bring democracy to Mexico.

IMPORTANT EVENTS IN
THE LIFE OF BENITO JUÁREZ

1806   Benito Pablo Juárez is born on March 21 in the village of San Pablo Guelatao, Mexico.

1828   Benito Juárez graduates from a religious seminary after seven years of study.

1831   Juárez begins working as a lawyer.

1843   Benito Juárez marries Doña Margarita Maza.

1847   Juárez becomes governor of the state of Oaxaca.

1855   After a revolution against Santa Anna, Juárez becomes the country's minister of justice.

1857   Mexico's Constitution of 1857 is signed. Juárez becomes head of the country's Supreme Court.

1858   Juárez is sworn in as president of Mexico. He begins the War of Reform against the Conservatives, who control the government in Mexico City.

1867   Juárez's army manages to force France to withdraw its troops from Mexico. Emperor Maximilian is executed.

1872   Benito Juárez dies of a heart attack in Mexico City one year after the death of his wife.

FIND OUT MORE
ABOUT BENITO JUÁREZ

Benito Juárez by Jan Gleiter. Milwaukee, Wis.: Raintree, 1990.

Benito Juárez by Dennis Wepman. New York: Chelsea House, 1987.

FIND OUT MORE
ABOUT MEXICO

Mexico by Karen Jacobson. Chicago, Ill.: Childrens Press, 1982.

Mexico by Ian James. New York: Franklin Watts, 1989.

Mexico by Richard Widdows. Englewood Cliffs, N.J.: Silver Burdett, 1988.

Mexico in Pictures by Department of Geography, Lerner Publications Company Staff. Minneapolis, Minn.: Lerner, 1988.

Take a Trip to Mexico by Keith Lye. New York: Franklin Watts, 1982.

INDEX

Page numbers in *italics* refer to illustrations.

jB
JUAREZ

De Varona, Frank

Benito Juarez,
President of Mexico

472105

12.40

DATE			